ITALIAN HILLTOWNS
NORMAN F CARVER JR

ITALIAN HILLTOWNS

NORMAN F CARVER JR

DOCUMAN PRESS

ACKNOWLEDGEMENTS

A work such as this owes most to the hundreds of friendly Italians who opened their homes, posed for pictures, guided my way, or brought to my attention unknown places. The initial impetus for this book began with friend and fellow photographer Balthazar Korab. He made several exploratory trips on his own or with me and his help was invaluable. The editorial skills of Harry Randall have been essential in keeping the writing on course—no simple task. Doris Barnes lent much in the way of enthusiasm and encouragement to bring the book to completion. And the staff at Morgan Press were unusually cooperative and skillful in the printing of the photographs. To all these, and the others who have given assistance and advice during the long gestation of this project, my deepest thanks.

A special mention must be made of my wife, who when not accompanying me, kept an architectural practice going and gave vital help in the editing and selection process.

Documan Press, Ltd.
Post Office Box 387
Kalamazoo, Michigan 49005

LCN: 79-63738
ISBN: 0-932976-00-9 Cloth
ISBN: 0-932076-01-7 Paper

Designed by Norman F. Carver, Jr.
Printed by Morgan Press, Inc.
Dobbs Ferry, New York
Printed in the United States

I affectionately dedicate this book to D.U.D., who over the years has consistently encouraged my photography and the documentation of vernacular architecture of which this book is a part.

CONTENTS

PREFACE

The Italians have built some of the most humane cities in the world. The archetypes for these cities were the villages and towns where, free from intellectual and stylistic pressure, the admirable fit between Italian life and the Italian landscape evolved. The purpose of this book is to document these villages and towns in part because they are inherently beautiful, in part because their unique character is in danger of destruction, and in part because their solutions to universal problems are in so many respects worth emulating.

My presentation is primarily visual, for in documenting architecture photography is a thousand times more effective than the clearest written description—though in the past, the photograph was seldom taken as seriously as the written word by critics or the public. Fortunately, this prejudice appears to be dying out, perhaps in the belated realization that the creative process is largely a recombination of visual images that can arrive at ideas and solutions outside the realm of purely verbal thinking.

The photograph can be a vital link in this process, because we think visually by drawing on a vocabulary of stored images acquired by indirect as well as direct experience. This book expands that vocabulary with images of a responsive man-made environment. And, although photographs involve only the sense of sight and cannot replace the total experience of moving through an actual place, their inherent selectivity focuses attention on the essentials of that experience—in this case the characteristic forms and spaces of Italian hilltowns.

I have made these photographs with a photographer's eye as well as an architect's eye. That is, I have tried to make them visually stimulating as well as informative. Though I have included a few of the larger and more famous towns, such as Siena and San Gimignano, which have adapted well to modern life, most photographs are of small anonymous towns that retain their original character. To convey as much as possible the original ambiance of these medieval places the photographs lie a little by what they leave out—you will see few contemporary signs, shops, electrical poles—though TV antennas appear with rather more frequency than I would have liked. The ubiquitous Italian automobile was less of a problem; the steep and narrow streets, never designed for any wheeled vehicle, force it to remain on the outskirts of the smaller towns.

Politically, culturally, and architecturally there are two Italies: the North, extending from the alps to about half way between Roma and Napoli; and the South, including the islands of Sicily and Sardinia. Within each region I have tried to show the range of characteristic types of images gathered from a variety of places. Occasionally, where a town was sufficiently interesting and unspoiled, I have shown it in some detail. I apologize to the connoisseurs of Italian hilltowns if I have slighted some favorite place. I only hope that as compensation they will discover in my photographs some new delights.

FOLK ARCHITECTURE —FORCES AND FORM

Folk architecture's distinction is that it developed without pretense to elegant style or heroic form, growing instead out of the practical needs of the inhabitants and the formidable restraints of site, climate, and pre-industrial society.

Such architecture has also been called indigenous, produced or living naturally in a locality; anonymous, bearing no name or of unknown authorship; and vernacular, belonging to or used by a particular people, or characteristic of a locality. More recently, it has also been called, polemically, "architecture without architects."[1] I have used mainly the terms 'folk' and 'vernacular', but for me they include all the above shades of meaning.

Folk architecture, as opposed to high-style architecture, has always been the dominant building type in any era and yet it was almost totally ignored by historians until, quite recently, perceptive critics began to contrast its virtues with the largely unfulfilled promise of modern architecture to "build in the nature of man."

This failure has compelled us to reexamine the foundations of modern architecture and planning. In the process our interest has shifted from traditional sources of inspiration—the palaces, cathedrals, and the monumental cities of the past—to simple, anonymous houses and villages which developed outside the established canons of style and taste, and which appear, in many instances, to have met human needs more successfully.

Such success was no doubt due in part to the restricted choices and the simpler building requirements of early societies. Even so, folk forms are instructive because they were a direct response to familiar and pressing personal or social needs and to the demands of climate or site. Their freedom from the 'artificial' restraints of taste or style enables us to more readily perceive how these fundamental forces shape our own man-made world. Italian hilltowns are especially rewarding examples for in them we may experience still-functioning models of "the extension of collective behavior into built forms".[2]

Unfortunately, their continued functioning is threatened by the social upheavals of modern industrialization and communication. Where many of these towns remained almost unchanged for centuries, at the present rate of destruction and abandonment, within a generation they will survive only in photographs. Their only salvation may lie in a world forced by rising populations and dwindling resources to once again adopt folk architecture's spare and simple forms.

Vernacular architecture, whether a single house or whole village, provides us with uniquely clear examples of the interaction between behavior, form, and the natural environment. For example, the igloo, critical to Eskimo survival, was built of the only available building material—packed snow—in an efficient structural form that resisted the winds, reduced heat loss through minimum surface, and grew stronger with use as the snow blocks solidified. Coping with the close quarters inside the igloo through long winter nights required singular social customs. Probably there has been no more precise and delicately balanced integration of culture, environment, and building form. In our increasingly vulnerable world the ways in which environment, culture and form interact are critical, if not to our survival, then to our quality of life.

There are barriers to exploring the forms of another time and another culture, however. The first barrier is cultural distance. Cultures which have disappeared or have radically changed deny us the chance to immerse ourselves in them, even momentarily.

Cultural distance can be both a hindrance and a help. It is a hindrance when it prejudices or clouds our perception of an architecture's practical or symbolic aspects. But then, even the inhabitants may not understand why traditional forms were built as they were, any more than they can explain the grammer of their spoken language. Their forms—verbal or three dimensional—are 'right' because they have always been so.

Cultural distance is a help, then, when it allows us to perceive aspects of form undetected by those intimately involved: "A cultural and temporal distance, by divesting architecture of its day to day practical and representational life, heightens abstraction and (thus) aids in the direct perception of form."[3]

Some investigators claim that most folk architecture is so shrouded in a complex and alien symbolism that outsiders can never make sense of its forms. While this may be partially true, it ignores two important points: first, all architectural forms can be and often are highly symbolic, even 'distorted' to purely symbolic ends. The mere act of building is an act of faith and thus symbolic. No forms are purely functional—even bridges and airplanes are, in spite of themselves, powerful symbols. It is, then, a universal tendency, and not

Captions for the photographs are opposite the first and last page of each photographic section. Other photographs of the same place are noted in the parenthesis.

A PHOTOGRAPHIC INTRODUCTION TO ITALIAN HILLTOWNS

9 The elemental, almost abstract quality of Postignano's buildings gives this tiny village a monumentality far beyond its size.

10 The two symbols of power in medieval Italy—the church and the castle, anchor opposite ends of Revello to its hilltop site south of Napoli.

11 Built to defend a river valley, this northern castle near Aosta fits its site so that the man-made forms seem like natural elements in the landscape.

Captions continued on page 25

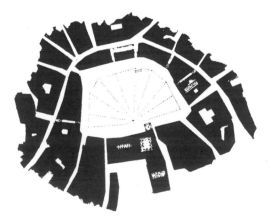

12,13 Siena has preserved much of its medieval character by controlling architectural changes ever since the 14th century when edicts were issued regulating the facades of the buildings on the Piazza del Campo. One enters the Piazza from narrow side streets which open dramatically onto one of the world's great urban spaces, always alive with people, and at the very heart of Sienese life.

14   The Italians seem to enjoy their public spaces more fully than most other peoples. As here in Perugia, the streets become a kind of theatre, particularly late every day, when strollers fill the streets and piazzas to see and be seen.

14   Fountain along one of the arcaded streets of Asolo.

15 *Firenze is a pedestrian city and a city filled with glorious architecture, so that the little dramas of daily life are often played out against monumental backdrops.*

16 *Venezia, with the Piazza San Marco in full swing.*

18,19 Characteristic of Italian hilltowns is their exploitation of dramatic sites and their compact forms set in the midst of unsullied landscapes. The southern town of Grisolia, and the northern town of Latera.

20,21 *The white towns of the south are usually bright, cheerful, and lively places. The dark, unstuccoed stone of northern towns, particularly at dusk, gives them a more somber, even gloomy mood.*

22,23 *There were no preconceptions in vernacular form — it evolved to meet local needs and conditions. The results could be as unusual as these trulli houses that make use of the abundant limestone slabs in one area of southeastern Italy, or as inviting as this passage that winds its way among the houses and rocks of Sperlonga's precipitous site.*

outside our own experience.

Secondly, primitive societies seldom set out to erect purely symbolic forms—the symbolism evolved from the original imperatives of providing secure shelter, whether for themselves or their gods. The thatched roof, for example, a widely used practical element in folk architecture, has always posed the difficult problem of securing and sealing the thatch at the roof ridge. Elaborate solutions to this problem provided the opportunity for highly visible symbolic elements distinctive for each locality. Similarly, church bell towers, which began as a practical means to announce the call to prayer, developed into the highly exaggerated towers that now symbolize "church." Evidently, an understanding of a form's practical origins can provide insights into its symbolic meaning.

Some investigators attempt to solve the problem of cultural distance by endless measuring, recording, and categorizing of "data" as if the sheer density of facts will somehow reveal their underlying meaning. But as useful as much of this information may eventually be, it is seldom possible to organize it in a manageable way so that its coherence can be perceived.

A more insidious barrier to understanding is the tendency to romanticize exotic cultures. It is almost impossible to avoid entirely, for we are able to wander through these places exempt from the day to day struggle to survive, charmed by the play of light and shade on quaint forms. But unrestrained romanticism is treacherous, as when Rudofsky mars his otherwise valuable discoveries by such comments as, "instead of trying to conquer nature as we do, (the inhabitants) welcome the vagaries of climate and the challenge of topography."[4] The inhabitants, of course, did not "welcome" challenges, they dealt with them as best they could, building on remote hilltops not because they welcomed a challenge to themselves, but because it posed a challenge

24 Bonifacio's spectacular site is on the southern tip of Corsica. Though no longer Italian, Corsica was a province of Genoa for hundreds of years.

Captions continued on page 32

25

to their enemies.

Our fascination with the picturesque qualities of folk architecture reinforces this romanticism. But we are made uncomfortable by picturesqueness because it has come to imply something contrived, quaint or artificially irregular—characteristics modern architects regard as immoral.

The dictionary definitions of picturesque suggest something quite different—images in which we could genuinely delight: "suggesting a picture; a wild or natural beauty; pleasantly unfamiliar or strange; quaint; informal; striking; vivid"—the very qualities that create the variety, surprise, contrast, and humanity so lacking in much recent architecture. A more likely reason for our discomfort with the picturesque is our suspicion that it is superfluous—that it has no functional importance. But only the narrowest definition of functionalism could exclude it, for if the mind truly delights in such qualities or if, as much evidence seems to suggest, the stimulations of variety and contrast are essential to a healthy mind, then any comprehensive definition of functionalism must include such psychological satisfactions.

Before a puritanical modernism made it a term of derision, the picturesque was a natural attribute of architectural form and of the man-made landscape, but decades of suppression dulled our skills in its use—even while demonstrating its indispensability. An important lesson of vernacular architecture, then, is that picturesque qualities of architectural form need not be contrived; they can logically derive, for example, from a sensitive adaptation to the site or from a forthright use of materials and building techniques.

It is impossible to deny the picturesque charm of Italian hilltowns—perhaps the most palpable aspect of their appeal. But beyond picturesqueness are characteristics which meet other fundamental human needs, and are, as we shall discover, not accidental or unique to Italy.

Forces and Form

I have used two terms, 'force' and 'form' in discussing vernacular architecture. By force I mean those natural powers, human needs, and cultural demands that influence the ultimate physical shape of the built environment. By form I mean all the physical attributes of this environment—its shape, spaces, color, and texture.

Vernacular architecture, because of its exceptionally thorough resolution of them, helps us to understand how various environmental and behavioral forces modify and are modified by architectural and urban form.

Unlike natural forms, man-made forms contend with only part of the forces present in their environment. To the extent they fail to contend with existing forces these forms will be unstable and unsatisfying. The neglected forces do not disappear; their effects eventually surface. The force of gravity, if not resolved by a building's form, exerts a stress that may be resolved ultimately by the building's collapse—just as an unfulfilled sense of security may lead to feelings of anxiety or eventually mental collapse.

Total resolution of all the forces affecting the man-made environment is, of course, impossible (and may not even be desirable, given man's apparently insatiable need for challenge). The stress of unresolved forces on both form and inhabitants is a constant goad for change. This has been particularly true during the last one hundred years, when the introduction of new materials and technology permitted a significant improvement in the physical comfort of our buildings. Unfortunately, this improvement has apparently been at the expense of increased psychological stress—our air-conditioned nightmare.

Some early peoples evaded the problems of building by living in caves or other natural shelters. But for most societies, building was a major focus of social energy. Shelter from excessive heat and cold and a secure place to work and rest were the initial impetus. Even initially, buildings and towns had broader uses—from facilitating community and family relationships to advancing a group's economic, political and religious life. The built environment thus materialized the social process in becoming the primary symbol of a culture's structure, values, and aspirations; "for the buildings speak and act, no less than the people who inhabit them; and through the physical structures of the city past events, decisions made long ago, values formulated and achieved, remain alive and exert an influence."[5]

Vernacular forms were shaped by an enigmatic and complex mix of forces— physical, biological, psychological, cultural— unique to each place and time. The resolution of these forces, complicated by rugged sites, harsh climates, or limited materials, was imperfect. However, through long periods of development there was time for a gradual adaptation of form to behavior, behavior to form, and both to the environment, finally arriving at workable if not utopian solutions.

Vernacular builders had no magic insights, only different attitudes. Where modern societies move rapidly from innovation to innovation, early societies developed pragmatic solutions over longer periods of time. Where modern societies are increasingly disparate and compart- mentalized, early societies were close-knit, with feedback between builder and user (often the same person). Where modern societies either slavishly follow or totally reject traditional forms, in early societies succeeding generations were influenced by variations of traditional forms motivated by real needs restrained by limited means and by the force of tradition.

Determinants of Form

Three groups of forces—physical, socio- cultural, and psychological—determine our built environment. In vernacular architecture the physical forces such as climate, gravity,

materials, and technology were the most direct and obvious in their effects and are the most measurable—even after a culture disappears. Therefore, it is these physical forces—direction of the sun and wind, amount of rainfall, or the availability of wood—that are most often invoked in describing each peculiarity of shape.

The availability of materials was the most basic determinant of form—in the sense that the materials at hand allowed, encouraged, or prevented certain solutions. In an area with little timber but with ample supplies of stone, we would expect to find stone-vaulted roofs rather than wide-span flat roofs. This is what occurred in Southern Italy, where the ground was covered with thin slabs of limestone that had to be removed to till the meager soil—the distinctive cone-shaped trulli houses were constructed entirely of this on-site material and were a natural outgrowth of its structural capabilities (144-151).

Socio-cultural forces, on the other hand, are generally more subtle in their effects and, especially in a dead culture, much more difficult to measure. Consequently, except for some obvious functional relationships between form and social organization—such as the effect of family structure on room arrangements in a house—the effects of a culture's attitudes, aspirations,and prejudices are typically either ignored or relegated to minor influence.

The relative importance of physical and socio-cultural forces in vernacular building depends in part on the environment. Under harsh conditions—the Arctic or the Sahara for extreme example—physical forces are the most powerful determinants, while a benevolent environment allows greater cultural influence on form.

However, even under severe desert conditions cultural traits have their effect. The pueblos of the Southwestern United States and the kasbahs of the Southern Atlas in Morocco evolved in remarkably similar environments using similar materials and construction techniques. Thick adobe walls and flat roofs in clustered cube shapes make the similarity of the village forms striking. But there are significant, culturally related differences. The pueblos of the Southwest, reflecting their more communal social activities, turn outward with access and entrances on the exterior, and with central plazas as meeting places for the community members. The Islamic 'pueblos,' are inward looking, with the house interiors, and family, sequestered from strangers and from the community.

Conflicts between cultural and physical needs may also result in seemingly "irrational" solutions. The Japanese disdain for physical comfort, exemplified in the samurai code, may explain their willingness to endure drafty, bone-chilling houses in the winter in order to open them wide during sultry summers (or was stoicism bred by houses inherently drafty?). The lightweight and flexible walls that satisfied this need in turn required social customs enabling the Japanese to cope with the extreme lack of privacy.

Of all of the forces affecting house or village form perhaps the most critical, but the most subtle, and still the least understood, are those imposed by the psychological needs of the individual and the society. We know, for instance, that an individual's sense of well-being, security, outlook are all affected by the built environment, but we do not know how and to what degree it is affected. One difficulty is man's ability to remain reasonably healthy in diverse psychological environments—making direct relationships between psychological forces and form extremely hard to define.

In addition, man's psychological needs are not static but changing—even contradictory—requiring an environment that alternates between:

> clarity and ambiguity
> privacy and affinity
> simplicity and complexity
> familiarity and uniqueness
> unity and variety

It is one of folk architectures' virtues, as opposed to much recent building, that it readily accommodates, even nurtures these diverse needs.

Vernacular forms, then, are not arbitrary but highly rational solutions to the complex problems of shelter. It is an organic rationality—organic not only because of the use of natural materials or because of the reflection of the natural environment, but organic because, like natural plant forms, the vernacular integrates a wide sphere of environmental forces.

Characteristics of the Vernacular

Considering the disparity of cultures, climates, and materials, the world's vernacular architecture would seem unlikely to reveal any consistent characteristics. Yet there are consistencies—reinforcing the conviction that vernacular forms reflect fundamental human and environmental conditions. Even apparent differences can reveal an underlying consistency. In Edward T. Hall's study of widely varying requirements for personal space among the Americans, British, and Germans, what was persistent and general were not the specific requirements, but the apparently universal need to define personal space.[6]

My list of such characteristics (there are undoubtedly others) has been gathered from a number of sources and from personal observations in a variety of settings. Taken as a whole, these characteristics define an architecture which is the very antithesis of high-style architecture—for they are not imposed intellectual concepts, but the outgrowth of real needs tempered by the building process, by the environment, and by the possible. Their universality may explain the vernacular's remarkable adaptability to varying cultures and times, and may also be the basis of a universal language of form by which we can discover our continuity with the past and enrich our future.

The characteristics that follow can, therefore, be seen as design principles serving the whole man—a way for making places "both beautiful and good."

Vernacular Forms Characteristically Show:

1. Functional motivation—both physical and psychological. The houses and towns were a direct response to the region's climate, building materials, culture, and individual needs. Variations in form reflected unusual conditions of siting or use such as those exceptional buildings developed for religious, governmental, or defensive use.

2. Precise adaptation to the climate. Without the technical means to ignore climate, vernacular forms developed simple, direct, effective means to moderate its effects—clusters for warmth in the winter, thick walls to retard the sun's heat in summer, narrow streets for shade, living space over animal quarters for warmth, openings towards summer breezes, blank walls toward winter winds.

3. Exploitation of the site and its variations. Unable to flatten all obstacles on a site, builders capitalized on its features—placing a castle on a high, easily defended rock, fitting houses among rocks or incorporating the rocks in walls—in the process developing variations on a unified theme that enhanced the richness of the living environment.

4. Close relation to and minimal impact on the environment. The immediate environment on which the community's livelihood depended was enhanced by compact settlements that preserved the land and, by the use of natural materials, integrated architectural forms with their surroundings.

5. Reflection of the building process and reliance on local technology, skills, and materials. Though occasionally incorporating foreign innovations, limited communications or means to transport materials any distance encouraged the use of what was immediately at hand—both materials and technical knowledge. There was no desire to make humble materials look expensive or to hide the way they were assembled, so the resulting forms had a directness to which everyone could respond.

6. Production by the whole community from a common tradition. The forms were not dictated by taste or a few specialists.

7. Variations in detail, but not in type. Because the tradition was adaptable to a variety of conditions the general scheme was already agreed upon when building began—details, size, placement on site were variable so that each building was familiar yet unique. Variations were limited to those based on proven functional needs. Novelty was atypical. Variations were unselfconsciously irregular—not for effect but for need.

8. Ornamentation functionally derived. Most symbolic and decorative elements grew out of solutions to functional problems that required special attention or effort, and gave some room for inventiveness without radically affecting the basic tradition.

9. Transcendence of the general pattern over the individual, repetitive, and elemental building units. Houses were not unique expressions. Their similarity and uniform density, interrupted by few exceptional buildings, created the rhythmic patterns of the overall form. The building types required were few— a headman's house, a temple, and peasant homes—usually packed to maximum density allowed by house type and the communication network. The few community buildings or spaces were sometimes sited symbolically, such as a church placed at an elevated point, but also accidentally.

10. Growth by slow stages and open-ended composition. Without a formal conception or rules of composition, additions could be made incrementally without affecting the overall scheme. The accidents of history were preserved in the town form.

11. Limited size and a consistent human scale. Limited size meant easy contact with the natural world just beyond the edge of the town and a preservation of comprehendable scale. Buildings, streets, and squares were sized for human use—only in the temple did the scale sometimes reach super human proportions.

12. Vivid overall form. Though built of natural materials and conforming to the contours of the site, the man-made forms, by their distinct geometry and uniqueness of silhouette, marked out a precarious but special place where man was in control.

The concerted effect of these characteristics was to create a unified environment of intelligible variety and authentic complexity. Some of the characteristics naturally are the result of the limited needs and capabilities of pre-industrial societies in which building types were few, and the technology for radical change unavailable. Traditional forms now disappear because of the increasing complexity of required building types; the increasing exposure to a variety of ideas that destroy the shared values necessary to support a tradition; the increasing pace of change without time for the evolution of traditional forms to meet new requirements; and because a growing technology makes the older forms no longer seem adequate.

Perhaps if the world holds still, we may develop new traditions of architectural form more comprehensive and nurturing than what we are now destroying—but one thing is clear, we shall never pass this way again.

But if it is only a small town, or fortification, it will be better, and as safe, not for the streets to run straight to the gates; but to have them wind about sometimes to the right, sometimes to the left, near the wall, and especially under the towers upon the wall; and within the heart of the town it will be handsomer not to have them straight, but winding about several ways, backwards, and forwards, like the course of a river. For thus, besides that by appearing so much longer, they will add to the idea of greatness of the town, they will likewise conduce very much to beauty and convenience, and be a greater security against all accidents and emergencies. Moreover, this winding of the streets will make the passenger at every step discover a new structure, and the front and door of every house will directly face the middle of the street; and whereas in larger towns even too much breadth is unhandsome and unhealthy, in a small one it will be both healthy and pleasant, to have such an open view from every house by means of the turn of the street.

But further; in our winding streets there will be no house but what, in some part of the day, will enjoy some sun; nor will they be without gentle breezes, which whatever corner they come from, will never want a free and clear passage; and yet they will not be molested by stormy blasts, because such will be broken by the turning of the streets. Add to all these advantages that, if the enemy gets into the town, he will be in danger on every side, in front, in flank, and in rear, from assaults from the houses.   *Alberti (ca. 1470)*

ITALIAN HILLTOWNS

With Italy's long history of conquest by foreign armies and bitter rivalry among its tribes, rulers, and city-states—to say nothing of roaming lawless bands—the countryside was a dangerous place. As a consequence defendable towns rather than isolated farms were the typical living pattern in Italy, and for that matter throughout the whole Mediterranean. The two Italies—North and South—though strikingly different in many respects, share this turbulent history.

The small Italian towns, with which we are mainly concerned, seldom have any recorded history. There may be a few faded documents kept in the church, some carved dates on tombstones or lintels, and a local legend or two, but little else to tell when the place was founded or how it grew. An inquiry about a town's age produces only a shake of the head and the comment, "all we know is that it is younger than Christ." We do know that some sites on the Italian peninsula have been continuously inhabited since at least the second millennium before Christ. Some, like Sorano in the North and Matera in the South were built over early cave communities—with the cave houses at Matera still in use well into this century.

From records that do exist it is evident that the most concentrated period of settlement and town building took place during the 11th to 13th centuries. It was a time of relative calm, but also a great period of castle building, especially in the South. In a process repeated over and over through the length of the peninsula, strong rulers or city-states expanded their territory by building fortresses on the frontier or beyond. These became the nucleus for new towns when citizens were encouraged or forced to settle beneath the walls and, together with the small garrison, defend the new territory.

The Site

Italy's mountainous terrain provided many dramatic hilltop or elevated sites, ideal for defense against marauding armies and protection from the malarial mosquitoes of the lowlands—a serious problem throughout the peninsula.

In addition, the use of hillsides, though it meant long steep climbs twice a day to the fields, preserved the limited agricultural land of the valley floors. Prominent sites also lifted the towns to the sun and air, and many towns oriented themselves to the winter sun along the south slopes (61, 108-109). The beauty of the spectacular views played little part in the choice if we judge by the few tiny windows opened to the views and the failure of many public piazzas to take advantage of the vistas (for an exception see Gubbio, 74).

Despite the tightly-packed houses and narrow streets, the smaller towns were not oppressive. There were numerous little piazzas within the security of the town, and always the release of the open countryside a few steps away.

Another practical aspect of the elevated sites was an automatic municipal waste disposal system. With no sewers or storm drains the rain water rushed down the streets collecting garbage, animal and human excrement. Other trash was dumped over the wall or out the window into the adjacent ravine—a convenient and not particularly harmful practice.

PHOTOGRAPHS OF NORTHERN ITALY

33 Built of and echoing the forms of the volcanic tufa site Vitorciano merges with its primal landscape (also 71-73).

34,35 Just inland along the Italian Riviera are a series of unspoiled towns perched on the south slopes of the mountains, facing the sun and the distant sea. Triora, Andagna, and Apricale.

36 In Triora five streets intersect in this vaulted space.

37 Arcaded streets of the small town of Zuccarello not only protect against the sun and rain but allow easy passage in a densely built up town.

39-46 Towns of the Val di Fafora, a magic valley near Firenze.

47 The linear village of Collodi extends from the Villa Garzoni up the single, steep street to the church.

48-55 San Gimignano.

56 Classic elements of the Tuscan landscape near Empoli.

57 Castlenuovo.

58,59 Arcidosso with Castel del Piano above.

60,61 Pitigliano's elevated site was protection against marauders and malaria.

62 Sorano from the west overlooking the river gorge.

64,65 Sorano's eastern slope.

66-68 Streets of Sorano and shoemaker's shop.

69 The village laundry, still very much in use, at Vieno Romano.

70-73 Vitorciano. (also 33)

74 Most medieval squares are surrounded on all sides. Gubbio's Piazza della Signoria, flanked on two sides by 14th century palaces, sits dramatically at the edge of the hill, one side wide open to a view of the valley below — the fourth side enclosed by the town rising up the hillside behind.

75 A small piazza in Spoleto and the street at the top of the staircase.

76,77 Valo di Nera.

78 Pierele's arrested growth is an opportunity to see the birth of a medieval town with a few houses huddled around a castle for protection.

79 Urbino is a sophisticated but small town whose towering Palazzo Ducale and cathedral are but a stone's throw from the open countryside.

Captions continued on page 113

Val di Fafora is a serene and tranquil place just west of Firenze. Seven small villages dot the wooded and vinecovered hillsides. On a Sunday morning in May, their stillness is broken only by the antiphonal echoing of church bells back and forth across the valley. (39-46)

Pontito, at the head of the valley, has a comparatively regular plan of gently curving, horizontal streets connected by steep stairways that radiate from the church piazza at the top of the village. (42-43)

The silhouette of San Gimignano emerging out of the golden Tuscan landscape is an unforgettable sight. Unlike some hilltowns, whose beauty is best appreciated from a distance, San Gimignano improves on close inspection. While only thirteen of its original fifty-six towers survive, its other special qualities remain intact. Just as in Siena, the ruder elements of the twentieth century have been restrained, if not altogether avoided. And like Siena it shows how the humane characteristics of medieval towns can absorb modern improvements such as adequate plumbing and electricity to provide a superb urban environment.

San Gimignano is a walled town of 5,000 inhabitants. Its famous towers, all attached to palazzi, were erected in the twelfth to fourteenth century as symbols of competing power among the nobility. Today, despite the tourists that descend on weekends, it retains during the week much of the flavor of a Tuscan country town, with its visiting farmers, its festivals, and its open-air markets. (48-55)

SCALE 1:5000

The whole village with its compact, hard-edged form symbolized a man centered world — a place where man appeared to control his destiny, no matter how tenuously, in the midst of an often hostile environment.

This strategic promentory has been
inhabited since Etruscan times and the tufa
walls of the river gorge are punctuated by
Etruscan and Roman caves. The present town
of Sorano, whose most inaccessible parts are
now partly abandoned, is a maze of slanting
lanes hewn out of the soft rock and lined with
houses that step down both sides of the hill
nearly to the river below. (62-68)

SCALE 1:2500

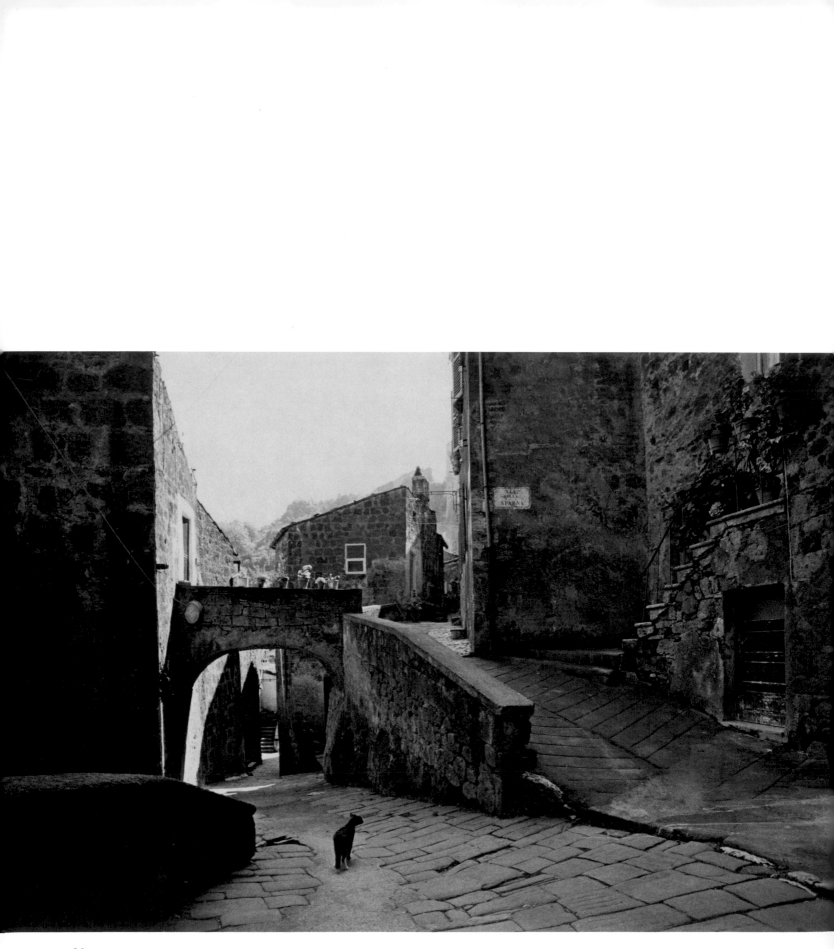

Vitorciano is another of the many villages built on volcanic rock outcroppings north of Rome. Its houses crowd to the very edge of the plateau, adapting and clinging to the natural rock formations. The stone of the houses is dark and mainly unstuccoed, creating a somberness only partly relieved by the unusual amount of interior greenery. (70-73, 37)

SCALE 1:2500

Though no substitute for walking through these towns, sequences of photographs can give some sense of the changing views, the variety of spaces, and the play of light and dark that one experiences in moving along the passages — one hesitates to call them streets. (75-76)

At the right, a sequence in Spoleto where a monumental staircase rises out of a small piazza and arrives, somewhat anticlimactically, at an off-axis archway leading to a quite ordinary street. (75)

During the half-century that precedes the Black Death the desire to make the city as a whole a thing of beauty at least begins, perhaps for the first time since Antiquity, to rival the importance of the need to make it strong against internal and external enemies. It is not merely that palaces grow more palatial and less fortress-like and multiply in number. The first tentative moves towards conscious, visual organization accompany a changing attitude to practical considerations, and the idea of town planning begins to take on a new meaning. The building or the reconstruction of a major church or palace becomes the occasion for a conscious effort to impose a certain visual order on the outcome of long centuries of unplanned growth. What had been a mystical ideal, an inarticulate urge, or an unwritten code begins to find a place in written regulations. However much the practical outcome may have fallen short of the intention, the theologians' ordered universe begins to find a counterpart not merely in the architectural symbolism of the individual church but in the shape of streets and squares. The first faint stirrings of ideas that flower in the formal concepts of the Renaissance are apparent. The desperate struggle for survival and salvation is slowly modified by more ambiguous attitudes. Increasingly, the organization of the affairs of this world rivals the hope of heaven as a social force.

John Edward White

3   4

2   1

From one of the lower streets that ring the town this passage winds upward towards the church at the top of Vallo di Nera. By a series of easy steps and ramps it passes through dark tunnels and sunlit turns until the church tower appears above. (76, 77)

Postignano is an archetype of the hilltown with its simple houses clustered around the defensive castle tower. Although now largely abandoned, it remains the spiritual center for the new village at the foot of the hill and the starting point for the annual church procession to a lonely chapel on a windswept hilltop across the valley.

The hillside site gives most of the houses access to light and air, even though they have been built, repaired, and added to apparently without plan — leaning against each other for mutual support. This easy irregularity, combined with consistent materials and forms, gives this small village a remarkable complexity and a compelling unity. (81-83, 9)

*One begins to realize how old the real Italy is,
how man-gripped and how withered. England is far
more mild and savage and lonely, in her country
parts. Here since endless centuries man has tamed the
impossible mountain side into terraces, he has quarried
the rock, he has fed his sheep among thin woods, he
has cut his boughs and burnt his charcoal, he has
been half domesticated even among the wildest
fastnesses. This is what is so attractive about remote
places, the Abruzzi for example. Life is so primitive,
so pagan, so strangely heathen and half savage. And
yet it is human life. And the wildest country is
half-humanized, half brought under. It is all conscious.
Wherever one is in Italy, either one is conscious of
the present, or of the medieval influences, or of the
far mysterious gods of the early Mediterranean.
Wherever one is the place has its conscious genus.
Man has lived there and brought the place to
consciousness, given it its expression, and really,
finished it. The expression may be Prosperine, or Pan,
or even strange "shrouded gods" of the Etruscans
or the Sikels, none the less it is an expression. The
land has been humanized, through and through: and
we in our own tissued consciousness bear the results
of this humanization. So that for us to go to Italy and
to penetrate into Italy is like a most fascinating act of
self discovery — back, back down the old ways of
time. Strange and wonderful chords awaken in us,
and vibrate again after many hundreds of years
of complete forgetfulness.*   *D. H. Lawrence*

The Apennines run the full length of Italy.
Among the highest are the Abruzzi mountains
east of Rome, where treeless, limestone peaks
alternate with high, isolated valleys. Life is
difficult and the climate forbidding for much of
the year so it is not surprising that many of the
villages have been partly abandoned as the
young people leave for the more promising
opportunities in the large cities. But a few still
cling to the old ways, farming the meager plots
in the valleys and grazing their flocks over the
rocky mountain sides. It is from these villages
that many fled to America early in the century,
but the village remained their ancestral home
and many have now returned in retirement.
(84-103)

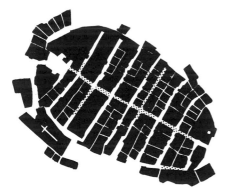

SCALE 1:2500

geometry that separates a village from the landscape in the sunlight becomes an indistinct mass blending with the hills in the rain. In the dim light, however, one unusually regular and compact pattern had caught our eye from the castle across the valley. Despite the clutter of recent additions, the original oval shape formed by the windowless houses of the outer wall was clearly evident. This was quite different from anything we had encountered thus far, so we crossed the lush green valley and mounted the opposite slope to the edge of the town. Gathering up our equipment before a few loiterers we entered the old part of the town —the central oval that we had seen from above —through a dark, unimpressive arch.

That arch led back several hundred years in time. Inside, the dark narrow streets of cobble were arched over by the second stories of the houses and lined with cantilevered stone steps shaped to permit the passage of loaded donkeys. It was baking day and women were gathering at the central village oven inside the gate, long boards balanced on their heads carrying the huge slabs of bread dough prepared at home. The smell of freshly baked bread filled the air. Other black clothed figures huddled under the arches to escape the rain.

The mood overwhelmed us. We felt like intruders and I set up as unobtrusively as possible to photograph a particularly handsome doorway. Just then the owner and his wife appeared, returned from the fields because of the weather. Pleased by my interest in their home but at the same time apologizing for its age, they posed momentarily in the doorway for a portrait.

A year later I returned to the village with a print of that portrait to present to the man and his wife. When I found him, he told me that his wife had died during the year. I could not tell whether he was touched by the gift, pained by the memories evoked by the image, or embarrassed by the informality of their dress, but he seemed only to glance at the photograph. He thanked me and, clutching the photograph under his arm, disappeared down the street. (92-97)

We approached Castelvecchio Calviso expecting only routine interest. We were now well into our second week of exploring the towns of the Abruzzi and becoming more selective about the towns worth our attention. The day grew increasingly dismal, an earlier dramatic storm having turned into a drizzle. Few hilltowns look their best under such conditions, but these dark rain-soaked walls and streets were especially bleak. The crisp

Repetitive forms that achieve artless and endless variety with simple means.

The effect of changing light on the reading of form is evident in the parallel rhythms of Pietra Secca. This steep village now is blessed with ready access to the autostrada, and these photographs, taken just two years apart, show the first of the insidious changes that will eventually destroy the unity of its forms and make of it merely another undistinguished place. (98-102)

These towns do not diminish the landscape,
they enhance it — they are themselves
crystallized landscape, growing out of the
natural materials and rhythms of the place.

81,82 Postignano. (also 9)

83 Postignano. The start of the annual church procession.

84 Against the awesome backdrop of the Abruzzi, Prata has an almost delicate quality. Built on the ridges of the hillside, its lines echo the underlying landscape.

86 San Stefano in the Abruzzi.

87 Calascio on baking day.

88-89 The castle above Calascio as an afternoon thunderstorm breaks.

90,91 Interiors of an abandoned house at the castle of Calascio. Vaulted roofs are common due to the shortage of wood timbers.

92 Castelvecchio Calviso from the castle of Calascio across the valley.

93 The main street of Castelvecchio is narrow, dark and arched over for much of its length by the second stories of the houses.

94 The steps, shaped to permit passage of loaded donkeys, lead to the living quarters on the second floor above the animal and storage areas.

95 A couple, just returned from the fields, in the doorway of their home.

96 Main street in Castelvecchio.

97 Bringing bread dough to the central oven for baking.

98,99 The abstract geometry of Pietra Secca's houses changes with the light.

100 Pietra Secca. The men take the sun in the main piazza while the women, separate as always, gossip and knit in the street outside their houses.

101,102 The streets of Pietra Secca.

103 House in Colli di Montebone.

104,105 Pereto and a detail of its castle.

106 The small barns on the edges of villages, because of their simplicity and smaller scale are a transition from town form to landscape. Orvinio.

107 Vallinfreda with Vivaro beyond.

108,109 The spectacular setting and unspoiled atmosphere of Anticoli Corrado have made it a favorite summering place for nearby Romans. The steepness of the hillside gives each house access to the light and the view, but typical of most hilltowns, only a few small balconies and windows exist to make use of them.

110 Monte Rubiaglio.

111 Caprancia.

112 Near Frascati south of Roma.

Captions continued on page 120

Town Form

The consistent use of hilltop sites covered with densely packed, stone buildings gave many towns a similar character. But infinite variations in the sites, the use or lack of walls, the siting of the castles and churches, and local variations in materials or details made each town unique—yet familiar.

In spite of the endless variety and individuality of the spaces, the houses, neighborhoods, and the towns themselves, the underlying unity of form provided a sense of order increasingly important to the Italians, while allowing for the diversity and individuality inherent in the Italian character and in the Italian society (38-46, 58, 73, 99, 131).

Most towns grew without plan as irregular, accidental clusters of mutually supporting individual units, accommodating the peculiarities of each site (9, 62, 159). A small number of towns did have a planned overall form, usually defined by a wall or a wall-like perimeter—some of these were so unified and solid in appearance they were more like a single huge castle (92-97).

The streets, designed for pedestrian and animal traffic only, were a maze of curved passages running parallel with the hillside, crisscrossed by diagonal ramps or steep flights of steps, passing under and through buildings, and meeting in complex intersections that opened into dozens of tiny piazzas or emptying suddenly on the main square adjacent to the church or below the castle walls (66. 76, 101, 142-143).

The main square was the center of town life. Nearly everyone in the village had to pass through at least once a day to draw water from the fountain, to conduct some business with the patron or at the town offices, to attend mass at the church, to buy fresh vegetables at the open-air market, or to sit long hours in the sun engaged in endless discussions. Farmers drove their flocks or loaded donkeys through on the way to and from the countryside. It was here the religious festivals began. And it was the site of that evening ritual, the "paseo" when young and old, men and especially women and girls (carefully chaparoned) could safely socialize under public gaze—while segregated groups of young boys and girls eyed each other as they strolled around the square or out to the edge of town. With a window overlooking this space, the priest and the patron were privy to everyone's affairs (13, 14, 16, 52-53).

The defensive town took three main forms: houses gathered around the castle; the walled town; and the contained perimeter town.

A castle was essential for expanding settlements, for protecting established towns, for protecting trade routes and market towns, and was the means of political domination over the adjacent territory. With the countryside unsafe, the citizens clustered their houses below the castle walls, often on precipitous sites. Some castle towns like Pierele (78) never grew beyond that initial phase.

Usually the first major structure on a site, the castle took maximum advantage of the defensive possibilities—often the highest, least accessible point with a view of the surrounding countryside. The church too commanded a prominent site so that the huge bulks of the castle and church on their elevated sites dominated the towns and gave each its distinctive silhouette.

A castle's thick masonry walls and cavernous rooms made for cold and drafty living quarters. When life became more secure, the castle soon gave way to the fortified palace, whose first purpose was not defense but the comfort and glory of the inhabitants. The supreme example of such a palace town was Urbino, where the Duke Fredrigo transformed an impregnable fortress into an elegant palace that became one of the two or three most influential centers of the high Renaissance. (79)

The walled town, usually with a castle enclosed or incorporated in the walls, was most apt to develop at sites without strong natural defenses or where the town had spread beyond the castle's protection. The wall provided physical protection, but it was important also as a symbol of the town as a place of shelter, law and order—in contrast with the lawless countryside.

The building of the walls was often a community project, and in growing towns a constant drain on the treasury as they were repeatedly rebuilt and expanded to include the "suburbs." Firenze's third perimeter wall consumed a quarter of the town budget for 46 years beginning in 1284. It was a massive undertaking—five miles long, 36 feet high and 6 feet thick, with 73 towers and 15 gates—the most impressive of the time.

The contained perimeter town, because of the wall-like solidity and continuity of the perimeter houses, often has the appearance of a single huge building or megastructure. Unlike the haphazard plan of most towns, the need for an ordered perimeter and limited size required more organization of interior spaces. An outstanding example of this type is the Abruzzi mountain village of Castelvecchio Calviso (92-97), whose regular grid pattern and uniform house-type indicate it was built under a single conception.

Though the practical need to draw together for defense was an important generator of town form, the towns were not an artificial device reluctantly resorted to for security. Even more important in the long run, building a town was place-making—the psychological focus for a whole geographic area and a vivid symbol of man's power to control his destiny, as well as fulfilling his deepest social, political, and economic needs. Where defense may have been of paramount importance in initial site selection, the political, economic, and psychological advantages of a site were crucial to its future success.

Although most towns initially grew haphazardly, it would be incorrect to imply that all towns evolved entirely by some instinctual process without any concept of or concern for an overall order. As they increased in size and sophistication there was a strong tendency for a town to regulate growth, and especially aesthetics. The chronicles of the larger towns such as Siena and Firenze are full of references to council meetings, regulations, and petitions concerning the need to impose some order on the city, both to improve the established parts and control the growing sections. Regulations concerned the heights of buildings, the widths and projections into the streets, the types of shops allowed in certain areas, and the size or shape of doors and windows and the building materials permitted around a piazza. In every case the concern of these regulations was aesthetic—the desire of the citizens to make their town a more beautiful, ordered place of which they could be proud.

A concern this strong was not limited to large communities. The small towns too had their pride. But they did not have the money or the sophistication and were likely in the protective custody of a lord or large commune without the full freedom to act.

The aim of these regulations was not to impose an alien style dictated by a few intellectuals; it was to codify and organize established tradition. Their purpose was to preserve order and coherence in times of growing population and change by imposing a general harmony that still allowed for diversity in detail. "There is more beauty in diversity than when all things are the same." This enlightened attitude, the need for a consensus, plus the slow pace of development after the ravages of the plague, and the lack of the technology for wholesale change meant that the underlying "instinctive" form of most towns changed little—preventing a wholesale remaking of towns according to some abstract geometrical order that has become the norm for town plans since the Renaissance.

Village Life

While a casual view gives the impression

of great tranquility and easy sociability in the midst of beautiful, natural surroundings, there is a dark side to village life. It can be tradition bound, dull, parochial, suspicious of change and rigidly routine—broken only by an occasional festival or funeral. When beset by unending poverty it is not surprising that the young leave for the large cities or foreign lands; however, when there is work nearby, a connecting train or bus, electricity, and decent plumbing available, then young families willingly return to these small towns.

A sociability, apparently instinctive, helps the Italians to use their public spaces as few other people. Perhaps it is because their houses are cramped and crowded with large families but the streets and piazzas are used constantly and noisily—especially at the end of the work day when the main squares and streets fill with people strolling with friends for an hour or two (13-17). This love of a crowd is so instilled that even on vacations, modern Italians jam a few overcrowded resorts for two or three weeks, leaving other times and places nearly deserted. It would be interesting, but probably impossible, to determine if this sociability is the product of generation after generation bred in crowded houses in small villages, or is innate in every Italian. Most likely it is a little of both reinforced by a church that stressed fidelity to family and parish, and rulers that demanded loyalty to the community.

The Building Units

The simple houses that make up the complex forms of the Italian hilltowns are extremely basic solutions to the problems of shelter. Shared multistoried stone bearing walls with wood poles for floor and roof construction or, where wood was scarce, stone-vaulted roofs were the standard construction. Interior rooms were simple cubes of space with few external openings—a shop, barn, or work space on the lower floor with living quarters above. The stone walls reverberated every sound of large families living in the one or two rooms. Private interior gardens were the exception and only in the South was there much use of roof tops.

With mutually supporting houses packed tightly together, the village made efficient use of materials and environment since it enclosed the maximum of space with the minimum of surface and tempered by the mass of stone it provided an exceptionally stable interior climate. The deeply walled, narrow streets were effective barriers against the hot sun and winter winds. Limited land within the walls or on the hilltop and a willingness to live closely caused a compaction of buildings limited only by the minimal width of the streets and the practical heights of bearing wall construction. This resulted in a uniform density and pattern of house forms enhanced by the similarity of materials, color, and shapes. The resulting pattern recorded the inhabitants' choices and struggle for survival against their neighbors, against gravity, and against the environment.

THE IMMUTABLE NORTH

Except for the broad Po valley in the North, high hills and rugged mountains are on every Italian horizon. South of the Po River where the Appenines begin, the mountain ranges extend in a sweeping arc west to the French Riviera and down the 150 mile width and 700 mile length of the peninsula to the straights of Messina, which abruptly separates Sicily physically and psychologically from the mainland. In places the mountains rise steeply out of the sea. Elsewhere, especially in the North, there are wide coastal plains intensively farmed and populated. The most impressive concentration of towns is among the fertile valleys of Toscana and Umbria. But there are hilltowns everywhere. Even in the remote mountain valleys of the Abruzzi, with no visible means of support, there are villages that have been there for hundreds of years.

Central Italy, especially the area between Firenze and Roma, is among the most beautiful man-made landscapes in the world. Especially on a late spring aternoon, when the hills and valleys are bathed in a golden green light and on the hilltops above, silhouettes of hilltowns emerge from the haze that dims details and enhances the abstract geometry (49, 56). I say man-made landscape because the evidence of man's hand is everywhere and yet everywhere restrained. For such an intensively inhabited land, Italy, away from the industrial centers, is remarkably beautiful —an example of how preservation of the landscape is helped by the compactness of the towns. But the land has also been abused—the great oak forests that covered much of italy were long ago turned into charcoal and centuries of grazing by sheep and goats have prevented their return and fostered erosion.

On Italy's northern border the Alpine influence is strong with a tradition of wood and stone farm houses isolated or loosely grouped in villages. But immediately on descent from these Alpine slopes, the tightly packed Mediterranean towns appear—built of dark gray or brown stone and roofed with stone slabs or dark red tiles. It is a style, with significant local variations, that extends the whole length of the peninsula.

Regardless of a climate which ranges from the semi-tropics of the Riviera to the bitter winters of the Abruzzi Mountains, the architecture of the North is surprisingly uniform. True, mountain towns that must contend with the cold seem more compact with smaller openings, and warm coastal towns more open, but the differences are slight. The traditional heavy masonry may not have been the ideal construction material under all these conditions—although its massiveness mediated extreme changes—but it was the one material readily available anywhere on the peninsula. The overriding similarity of form can be partially explained by the limited building materials, but even more by the strength of a tradition that was established early in the more moderate climates, with defense as a prime motive, and then spread as much by force as by choice.

The uniformity of the northern building tradition and its generally high level of craftsmanship, combined with a traditional urban pride, makes northern towns much less subject to superficial changes than their

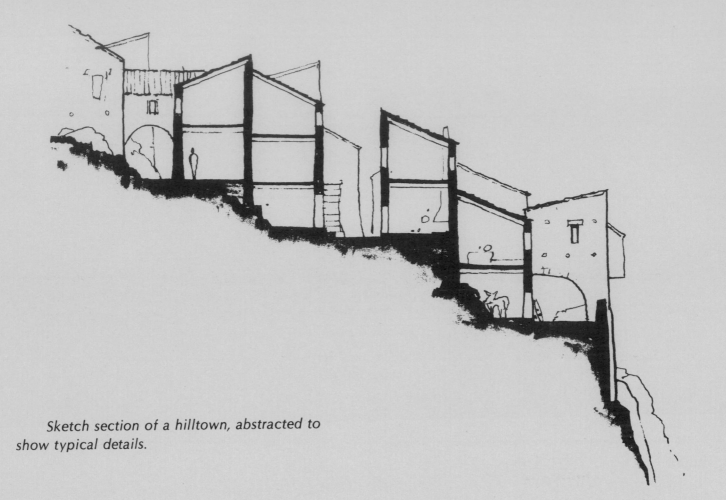

Sketch section of a hilltown, abstracted to show typical details.

southern counterparts. Indoor plumbing and electricity are introduced into fifteenth century towns with minimal evidence—while in the South such wonders are something to be flaunted.

Moreover, there is in the North a long standing practice of communal regulation of use and aesthetics—which at least in the larger towns retains some effectiveness. So the attempts at control are not recent or alien, but a concern that has been expressed for hundreds of years. Unfortunately, this attitude does not often extend to the small anonymous towns shown here, since appreciation of their value is recent and not shared by many—even the inhabitants, who sometimes asked how I could be interested in their "brute paese", their humble village.

Not all hilltowns were built on hills or even in the hills; however, elevated, defensive sites set the pattern for Italian towns so that even those built in valleys retain the compact hilltown form, usually surrounded by walls as a substitute for natural isolation. Some towns, such as Siena and San Gimignano, were built on hills so slight that they offered little physical protection. The conclusion is that there was something innate in the Italian or Mediterranean character that directed the building of towns on elevated sites whenever possible; considering the added problems of access to water and agricultural land, it was not an idle decision. Of course, not all towns are the result of a conscious decision—some simply expanded from an initial house or two placed without concern for its defensive potential.

THE INCONSTANT SOUTH

About half way between Roma and Napoli a subtle change begins, not so much in the landscape, but in the people and in their towns. Here begins another world—the second of "the two Italies." Travelers for a long time have passed it by as too remote, too dangerous, and too lacking in cultural monuments—so the South is not well known, even by Italians.

It has a diverse landscape, climate, architecture, and people. Its only apparent unity is the southerner's distrust and resentment of northern prosperity. Though fought for by foreign armies, the South has for a long time been ignored by the central government—so the southerner is suspicious of the northerner and distrustful of government bureaucrats and their programs and relies more on traditional systems of power.

This power derives from a southerner's desire "above all to be obeyed, admired, respected, feared and envied."[7] Such attitudes are not wholly compatible with the modern industrial state and the South has remained aloof from the intense industrial expansion in the rest of Italy. Isolation and poverty have made the southerner quick to adapt but slow to change and despite recent improvements, an immense poverty remains.

The landscape in the South varies from the green, rolling plateaus of Puglia in the southeast to the barren, treeless and dry plains in Sardinia and Sicily, to the fertile volcanic fields of Campania, and to remote mountains in Basillicata, Calabria, Sicily, and Sardinia. The climate changes according to the altitude and proximity to the sea, but in general, summers are hot and dry, winters mild and damp.

Except for a few prosperous oases, the South is much more thinly populated and impoverished than the North and the pace of life slower. Yet the South has produced some of Italy's greatest talents in the arts and some of its most important leaders—the people resiliant and resourceful from centuries of foreign domination, famine, earthquakes, isolation and neglect.

Partly because of the differing cultural influences—Greek, Arab, Norman, for example—and partly because of demands of climate or the limits of available materials, the forms of southern towns and houses are more varied than in the North. In extreme cases, they become almost African in feeling—as in the trulli of Apulia or on the small islands around Sicily.

Stone is the dominant building material, but the farther one proceeds South, the cruder this stonework becomes. There is also an increased use of stucco, perhaps to conceal the less skillful masonry. A drab grey or dirty tan, the stucco lacks the richness of color and texture of northern stone. The unstuccoed towns of the rough masonry are ragged in appearance—conspicuous for being lower and less compact than in the North. Perhaps this is due to lack of skill, to frequent earthquakes, or to poverty, but the effect when combined with the southerner's desire to make showy additions with his first touch of prosperity, is to increase the disjointed appearance of the towns.

121 Locorotondo.

123-125 Island of Stromboli—houses along the coast.

126 Sardinia. Ruins of pre-historic stone towers called nuraghi are found throughout the island. This type of round mortarless stone structure is still used today for simple shelters in many parts of the Mediterranean, and probably is the antecedent of the more elaborate trulli houses that developed in southern Italy.

127 Sardinia. A barn window plugged with stones to keep out birds.

128 Inland from Cefalu on Sicily's north coast.

129 Sicily. The similarity of house forms in Cimmina give it an interesting abstract texture, but in detail the houses and spaces inside the town are uniformly dull.

130,131 Sicily. Cefalu is built around the base of a huge rock that serves as its natural castle. The lack of space crowds the houses to the edge of the small harbor.

132 The varied landscapes of Sicily and Sardinia often surpass the towns in interest. These isolated farm houses are along the south coast of Sicily near Menfi.

134 A cemetary outside Pietraperzia with the aspect of a small village. The structures, more imposing than those of the town itself, are in keeping with the Sicilian desire for making an impression, even at the last moment.

135 Pietraperzia in central Sicily.

136 Vieste at the tip of the Gargano Peninsula. The coast in this area is lined with large fishing platforms made of lashed poles cantilevered from the cliffs from which huge nets are lowered into the sea.

137 A street of steps in Sannicandro including a small accommodation to the wheel down its center.

138-143 Ostuni.

144 Trulli houses in the Val di Itria near Martina Franca.

145 An unstuccoed interior of a trullo dome.

146 Trulli near Cisternino on the road to Ostuni.

147 This low dome—typical of early simple field shelters—incorporates steps to enable use of the roof for drying foods and an elegant downspout of stucco to lead the rain water into a small cistern. A house on the road between Cisternino and Ostuni.

148 Near Alberobello. Trulli cones are usually left unstuccoed on the exterior since the outer layer of stones act as shingles to shed the water. The peak is waterproofed by an exuberant bit of sculpted stucco varied slightly from house to house. The other whitewash decorations are splashed on as warnings to thieves, hex signs, or at the owner's whim.

149 Small farm house cluster near Martina Franca. Each peak covers just one room.

150 A street lined with trulli in the town of Alberobello.

Captions continued on page 185

*Forces generate form. In the case of certain
simple natural systems this is literally true; in the
case of man-made systems it is a metaphor. The forces
which are not provided for do not disappear. They
always find an outlet in an unexpected way. The
deeper psycological and social forces, if not provided
for, can easily have repercussions which lead to
drastic kinds of instability. They do not of their
own accord create a stable state.*

Christopher Alexander

The houses on the volcanic island of
Stromboli, off Sicily's north coast, have an
African feeling. The basic module is a simple
cube adapted to a variety of uses and clustered
to make one house or a group of houses. The
exterior of the clusters, with only tiny openings,
shelters from the relentless sun and wind while
within the houses open on small courtyards that
are private and protected. The small scale of
the cube module and the irregularity with
which it has been clustered and adapted to the
site create a strangely harmonious relationship
between an uncomprimising geometry and the
rugged landscape. (123-125)

Sicilian and Sardinian towns, in contrast with mainland towns, are usually without compact form or dramatic sites. Their original, rather ragged architecture is not enhanced by the addition of showy and superficial improvements in the Sicilian manner. An exception is Cefalu (130, 131) on Sicily's north coast, which is tightly packed between the sea and its castle-like natural mesa. (126-133)

The brilliant white town of Ostuni preserves its original walled perimeter nearly intact. Built on a low dome-shaped site at the edge of the Murge escarpment, a few miles from the Adriatic, its few exceptional forms — churches and official buildings of unstuccoed stone — rise above a cubist sea of whitewashed houses.

The town of 30,000 is an unusually clean and lively place. Both the streets and the rooftops are filled with activity. In the afternoons, while the men are at work, neighborhood women gather on the shady side of the street to sew and gossip, the children play, and the old men sit and doze. Then, in the early evening, with the stone walls amplifying every sound, all radios are turned up full volume, the houses and streets fill with people talking — no shouting — to each other, and Ostuni comes fully alive. (138-143,20)

In the heel of the Italian Peninsula conical stone house forms called trulli probably evolved from the simple stone field shelters found throughout the Mediterranean. Here the ready supply of appropriate stone encouraged the flowering of this form into complexes ranging from one house to whole villages.

The green and gentle landscape sprinkled with these exotic forms is a testament to the ingenuity and sensitivity with which man can shape his environment. (144-154, 22)

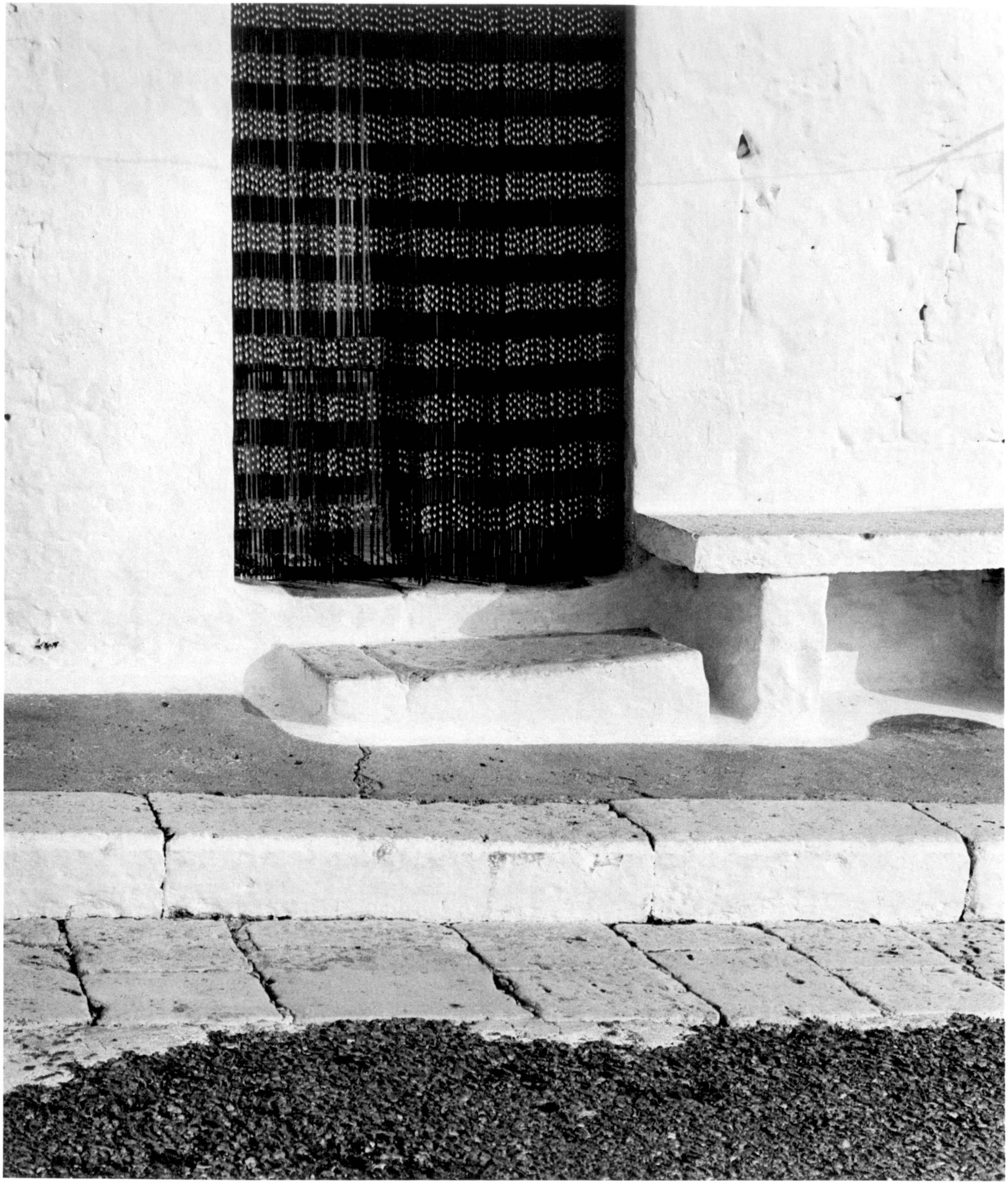

Locorotondo and Martina Franca are two attractive white towns where a variety of more conventional flat and vaulted-roofed houses of mortared stone were built in the midst of the trulli. In the densely packed, older sections stairs and passages along the narrow, shaded streets lead to multiple levels of habitation. (153-157)

High on their eroded hilltop, the inhabitants of Pisticci pay for their isolation with long arduous trips to the farms in the valley below. The town is composed mainly of a single story house-type that undulates in rows over the irregular site creating, instead of deadly uniformity, a rhythmic pattern of varied forms and spaces. (160-163)

The two towns of Grisolia and Maiera face each other across a deep crevice overlooking the Mediterranean. (170-173)

Sperlonga is a "southern" whitewashed
fishing village just a few hours south of Rome.
The whole town is now under government
protection to prevent the usual destructive
"improvements." The automobile penetrates
only to the little square at the top of the hill,
while a beautiful labyrinth of pedestrian
passages, stairs, and tunnels wraps around
three sides of the promentory. With the
addition of electricity and adequate plumbing
the houses have now become fashionable
weekend retreats for Romans and Neapolitans.

To satisfy a variety of functional needs the
solid shaped houses and the eloquent interior
spaces are unselfconsciously irregular, varying
only in detail not in type. The result is a village
form unique yet familiar, simple yet complex,
and diverse yet unified. (175-182)

SCALE 1:2500

151 Sections of Alberobello are now under government protection to preserve this uniquely handsome example of a trullo town.

152 Alberobello. Doorway of a house.

153 Cisternino. The owner shows the interior of her small home, emptied for repairs and fresh whitewash. The original simple trullo shape, now much remodeled, can still be detected.

154 In the heat of the day the streets of Martina Franca are nearly deserted, the residents prefering the cool interiors of their stone-walled houses.

155 A couple in front of their house in Martina Franca.

156 The southern facade of Locorotondo's round plan has been beautifully preserved.

157 In Locorotondo's older sections the narrow streets are often extended upwards by stair upon stair as houses were built one upon the other.

158 Older women in the South, more often than in the North, regularly wear the traditional clothing. One woman is spinning yarn from raw wool as she visits with neighbors in front of her house.

159 Craco.

160-163 The town of Pisticci.

164,165 A farm house just below Pisticci.

166,167b A steep street in Tursi and a neighborhood well at its top.

167t Houses on a prosperous farm near Pisticci.

168 The immaculate interior of a bachelor farmer's one room home near Pisticci. The owner,

justifiably proud of his home, asked to be photographed while praying to the image of the Virgin hanging at the head of his bed.

169 A farmer of Rocca Imperiale, after his noon siesta, heads again for the fields with his burrow.

170 The town of Grisolia stretches out along the ridge overlooking a small canyon. On the opposite ridge is Maiera, just visible in the lower left of the photograph. The canyon has served for centuries as a convenient sewer and garbage dump for both towns.

172 From Maiera a nearby abandoned village is silhouetted against the setting sun shimmering on the Mediterranean.

173 Grisolia and Maiera.

175-182 Sperlonga. An unusually well preserved town with many handsome passageways and small courts.

183 At the toe of the Italian boot is Pentadatillo on its ominous site.

EPITAPH

184t Progress at the edge of Martina Franca—a fate that awaits most Italian towns as insensitive speculation destroys the cohesiveness of town form.

184b With all the superb examples of town "planning" at hand even more appalling is the deadly rigidity and uniformity of this new, planned town in the Gargano area.

For example, the towns of Sicily and Sardinia lack the charm of an attractive house type, and compact form or are seldom interestingly sited. In addition, most buildings are new or remodeled creating chaotic color and form. It is often difficult to find any evidence of the original materials and forms now covered over with brightly colored stucco and sheets of plastic or corrugated steel.

Sardinian towns are especially uninteresting—lacking even the minimal unity of the Sicilian. Distant views, which can often make any place look attractive, reveal little overall order, and closer, they completely fall apart visually. Also, old street patterns have been modified into more regular grids to make them "up to date", destroying what little interest and diversity did exist.

The reasons for these radical changes are partly that the towns were not that fine to begin with—there was not that much worth saving. And partly the southern tendency to put any extra money into things that make the greatest impression—the most modern techniques or the most visible colors.

White towns are frequent—but not the hundreds of dazzling white towns as in Greece or Spain. Among the most attractive are Sperlonga, Pisticci, and the towns of Apulia (174, 161, 138-157).

Apulian towns—the trulli area—are some of the handsomest and most interesting towns in all of Italy. They are mostly small, white, and invariably immaculate. Some consist entirely of trulli—now much changed. Others, surrounded by a landscape full of trulli houses are built in more conventional form—as if disassociating themselves from the lowly peasant style. Though Apulia is one of the densest areas of scattered farm houses, small towns are plentiful—some no more than slight concentrations of trulli. As elsewhere in Italy, these towns were not systematically planned; instead, they expanded in conformance to the demands of nature and the needs of man. These were

Sketch plan and section of a typical trullo

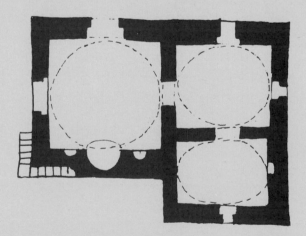

small agricultural towns. They did not aim for an artificial impressiveness of or follow an alien pattern of pretentious buildings and monumental spaces. Their impressiveness lay in the rhythmic repetition of a single house type, compact and dense, arranged to reflect the social realities of small town life. The overall form was vivid, varied, and modestly monumental.

Such spontaneous growth patterns encouraged strong, cohesive neighborhoods whose boundaries, invisible to the visitor, are real to the inhabitants. Citizenship in a small town or the neighborhood of a larger town commanded the southerner's loyalty and was a basis for their clannish self-sufficiency. Today even with land reform the habits of centuries do not change and most people prefer to live in the towns rather than be isolated in the countryside.

The extreme density of houses constructed in layer upon compact layer meant these relatively small towns sometimes held thousands of people (156,157). But the density was not oppressive—the ever present countryside, the informal street patterns, the intense light of the high whitewashed walls in narrow streets reflecting light into every corner or casting welcome shade in the heat of summer made these towns pleasant and vital places.

White towns, of course, are in stark contrast to the natural landscape—but surprisingly harmonious with it. They prove that an organic architecture does not require a gratuitous blending of architectural and natural forms but an understanding of the relationship of architectural to natural form. Here, for example, the geometry is softened by the infinite coats of white wash, by the small scale and by irregular distribution over the land so that in spite of its contrast the town never overwhelms—there is always the sense of the landscape with the works of man in it.

BIBLIOGRAPHY AND NOTES

A brief list of books that I found particularly helpful:

1   Rudofsky, Bernard. *Architecture Without Architects.* New York: Museum of Modern Art, 1964 (unpaged).

    Rudofsky's comments are sometimes extreme, but this collection of worldwide folk architecture was an important milestone.

2   Van Eyck, Aldo. (as quoted in the Student Publication, School of Design, University of North Carolina, ca. 1968)

3   Carver, Norman F., Jr. *Silent Cities: Mexico and the Maya.* Tokyo: Shokokusha, 1965 (p. 8).

    Comments and photographs on the architecturally significant sites in Middle America—seen as space and form rather than archaeology.

4   Rudofsky.

5   Mumford, Lewis. *The City in History.* New York: Harcourt, Brace & World, Inc., 1961 (p. 302).

    An exhaustive treatment of the classic cities and periods of western civilization including some perceptive observations on medieval towns. Excellent and extensive bibliography.

6   Hall, Edward T. *The Hidden Dimension.* New York: Doubleday & Co., 1969 (p. 131ff).

    A study of personal space including its architectural implications.

7   Barzini, Luigi. *The Italians.* New York: Atheneum, 1964 (p. 236)

    Insights into the Italian character, North and South.

Allen, Edward. *Stone Shelters.* Cambridge: MIT Press, 1969.

    Detailed study of the trulli and other stone structures of Apulia and nearby areas.

Automobile Club d'Italia. Various volumes in the Italian Itinerary Series.

Cornelisen, Ann. *Torregreca: Life, Death, Miracles.* Boston: Little, Brown and Co.

Devastating and moving account of life in a small southern town by an American who lived there for several years.

De Wolfe, Ivor. *The Italian Townscape.* London: The Architectural Press, 1967.

    Lively photographs and comments on urban details.

di Cristina, Luciana. *La Citta-Paese di Sicilia.* Palermo: dell'Universita' di Palermo, 1965.

Gutkind, E.A. *Urban Development in Southern Europe: Italy and Greece. International History of City Development, Vol. IV.* New York: The Free Press, 1969.

Larner, John. *Culture and Society in Italy, 1290-1420.* New York: Scribner's and Sons.

Lawrence, D.H. *Sea and Sardinia.* New York: Doubleday & Co., 1954.

    I am grateful for permission to quote (on page 85) the passage which so succinctly conveys the sense of history one feels constantly in Italy.

Moholy-Nagy, Sibyl. *Native Genius in Anonymous Architecture.* New York: Horizon Press, 1957. Pioneering work by a most perceptive architectural critic.

Rappaport, Amos. *House Form and Culture. Foundations of Cultural Geography Series.* Englewood Cliffs: Prentice-Hall, Inc., 1969.

    One of the best studies yet on the significance of folk architecture. Includes a complete bibliography.

Soavi, Giorgi. *Toscana.* Firenze: Marchi & Bertolli, 1967.

White, John. *Art and Architecture in Italy: 1250-1400. Pelican History of Art Series.* Baltimore: Penguin Books, 1966 (p. 159).

    My appreciation to the author and publisher for permission to use the quotation on page 75.

Waley, Daniel. *The Italian City Republics.* New York: McGraw-Hill.

INDEX

LEGEND

* For consistency the Italian spelling has been used for all place names, including Rome (Roma), Florence (Firenze), Venice (Venezia), and Naples (Napoli). References to photographs are in italics.

ITALY

•1

•MILANO

•5

6 •VENEZIA

•GENOA

•4 •3
•2

•7
•8
•9

10
•FIRENZE

•12

•13
•14

•11

•18
•17

•19
•15 •16 •20
•22 •21
•23 •27
•24
•25
•26

•37 •38
•28 •30 •39
•29 •31 •40
•33 •32
•ROMA •34
•35

•36

•42 •43
•44
•41

•NAPOLI

•45 •46
•48 •47
•50 •49

•53 •51
•52
•54
•57

•55
•56

•66

•65

•59

•58

PALERMO •64 •60

•63 •62

PHOTOGRAPHIC NOTES

The photographs in this book were selected from over 5,000 made during a ten year period beginning in 1967. Reducing this to the 175 photographs used in the book was an agonizing task, for much that was fascinating had to be omitted.

Italy is an especially enjoyable country to photograph both because of the wealth of material and because of the cooperative people who thoroughly enjoy being photographed.

In the decade this work covers many changes took place—almost none for the better. Towns that were photographed unscathed in the early stages now have raw new apartment buildings in their midst. Or new autostradas have ripped open the land and dumped hordes of cars and people onto unprepared villages and landscape—more changes in the last ten years than in the previous 100.

The photographs were made with Hasselbald cameras using lenses from 38mm to 500mm—some with 35mm Nikon and Olympus, 21 to 200mm lenses. Most photographs were duplicated in color. Films were Plus-x, Tri-x, and Ektachrome, developed in D-76 and printed on Polycontrast. Plates were made from these prints and printing of the photographs overseen by the photographer.

AVAILABILITY OF PRINTS:

Archival prints of any photograph in the book are available. Prints are personally made and signed by the photographer. A portfolio of 10 prints, 11x14 mounted on 16x20 museum board is also available. The 10 prints may be selected from the photographs on the following pages: 9, 15, 17, 23, 25, 45, 67, 89, 90, 95, 121, 127, 132, 144, 147B, 153, 164.

For current prices contact the photographer in care of the publisher, Box 387, Kalamazoo, Michigan 49005, USA.